Thousand-Year-Old Words

by
Nan Cohen

GLASS LYRE PRESS

Design & Layout: Steven Asmussen
Cover art: 26021679 | © Zigzagmtart | Dreamstime.com
Author Photo: Miri Henerson

Glass Lyre Press, LLC
P.O. Box 2693
Glenview, IL 60025
www.GlassLyrePress.com

Thousand-Year-Old Words

For Ellen Barber

CONTENTS

1

2

3

1

STRAND

A thousand-year-old word is a broken bowl,
a few sherds each as big as a dish,
uncountable fragments and dust.

I am stranded, its pieces strewn before my feet.

Each piece of the story is a strand.

A rope. A shore.

CLEAVE

A Janus word, it looks both ways.

And its faces are bound at the back of the head.

Some of its synonyms fierce Anglo-Saxon verbs
—*hew, chop, sever, rive*—

Some of its synonyms Latinate—*adhere, remain*—
but some are old in English: *hold* and *cling.*

When I think of it, I think first of a hatchet
descending in an arc to sever—a thigh
from a chicken?—and bury its edge in wood

And only after, of two joining hands,
fingers interlaced down to the webbing,
two bodies joined like split sticks

The two meanings align at the seam
saying anything whole can be halved
saying what is divided is not parted forever

despite the blow   the stroke   the sundering.

SHIMMER

A thousand-year-old word is a needle
pulling a thread that is centuries long.

A thousand-year-old word wraps itself
around a quality of light,

and like light itself seems ageless,
untouched by time.

Light travels through imperfect glass
into darkened rooms, but

moves with the same vigor;
a word may have taken in a trembling

it did not have a thousand years ago,
but all we can know is how it shimmers now,

wrapping itself around the ageless light.

It was how light found him:
that shimmer was the light's surprise.

And now of all the words I cast
toward the place he once appeared,

this is the one that wraps itself around
that emptiness, that absence where he stood.

WEEP

A thousand-year-old word is an ancient door
that keeps the dark inside a room of stone,

or keeps it out at night when the room is lit.
Though weapon and wolf are gone, it keeps out wind,

And keeps in what the room contains.
What does the room contain? What must be kept,

what furnishings, what dignity?
What is stitched into its hanging tapestry?

And what if I swung it wide, the door—
letting the dark inside be bathed in light.

Or bringing in the outside dark
to gather around the table, with a candle

still glowing on a weeping face,
and winking in the diamonds of its tears.

LOSS

A thousand-year-old word is a loosening, too.
The human hand opens eventually,
lets go of what it held.
A thousand-year-old word escapes the mouth,
the *l* rolls off the tongue, the vowel splays wide,
aww, the teeth close on a hiss, on nothing.

SPELL

You know that words have magic. Are.
That to pull you through time is one of their powers.

Gasp. As a noun, I learned, it was first recorded
in the year I was born. When I marveled at its newness,
I also felt my age. A gasp

is one way to describe how we move through time—
for another kind of pulling is that force,

among all the forgotten words, of the ones remembered:
I met someone. That's how you are. I'm sorry, he's already gone.

HOME

The throat shuts; a small emptiness opens.
A thousand-year-old word is a bite of air,

the thing itself, and the loss of it.
Like the door to a place we used to live,
the old paint peeling, or repainted green.

Haunt comes from *home*—
it's where the ghost goes.

LAST

Having once more chosen a trail to follow,
we have, once again, arrived:

where the trail ends
in the mark of roughly half a shoe.

If this were a detective story, I would say
he leapt to the right side

—here is a disturbance in the undergrowth.

His disappearance is two footprints,
is final, will be remembered.

WIND

Winters in LA, rain and wind clear the sky
to a startling blue. On the sidewalk,
fallen branches and drifts of brown leaves.

More people than you'd expect, perhaps—
out walking, alone, or with kids and dogs.
I went up the block, thinking of wind,

of the Pacific, twenty miles away,
of warm air rising from the playground blacktop
—our local desert—and, far beyond it,

the great deserts and plains of the West,
imagining wind rushing up and down
mountains, rolling into canyons in waves—

Can anyone tell where it begins and ends?
And then I saw them: a flock of green leaves,
in the diamonds of a chain-link fence,

all caught and fluttering next to the tree
the wind had loosed them from and in their trembling
saying everything I had thought to try to say.

2

SOUL

Of these poems, David asks, *Who is the "we"?*
    and I am stopped; this is a holy question.

For I had forgotten the small,
    the humble words that hold language together

like the hand-forged nails that held pieces of wood
    in the shapes of window frames through which

—at any moment in a thousand years—
    someone might look to see someone coming

up the path to the door.

HAND

I might see hundreds of them, any day
—and not see them, their tasks, their work;

might read the gestures they write on air
without looking at the hands themselves.

Even my own, now—
one lifts to rub the corner of an eye,

one waits, resting on its wrist.
Do they not appear grotesque?

Two fistfuls of muscle, tendons, bones,
bundled with flesh in these old gloves of skin?

Never mind that everywhere I've been, I've seen
one hand reach for another,

never mind whom my hands have touched or why.
When soon they rise to strike these keys,

I will not be thinking of my hands. I'll feel
no gratitude for them or their obedience.

KISS

An old poem taught me long ago:
One easily severs what never was joined.

But of moments in time I have this to say:
they have a way of joining,

and sometimes their severing mends them.

The way two people kissing briefly join,
then part. All is changed.

Our many partings,
seen from a distance, resolve;

the fragments make a pattern:
another old lesson, relearned.

GRIEVE

A year is big enough for a whole calendar of loss:
four seasons, major holidays, a handful of afternoons

when you look in the empty mailbox and down the street
before remembering: no deliveries today.

And small enough to find tucked between the pages
of an old book or in a jar of coins.

I used to think to grieve was a tall tree bending, the wind
that shook and flattened whole fields of long grasses;

now I think it's whenever the air stirs around us,
fierce or soft, bringing sometimes a burst of rain,

sometimes nothing, or only a light scrim of dust.

TABLE

What we never
told each other hung in
the air between us as much as
any

other
words we spoke, while
what was off the table
—I see now—was always on it,
a dish

of salt
between our plates
we could have dipped into.
Forgive me. We shared so much else.
Forgive

that I
break our silence
without you. Time rewrites
memories, so while I can I'll say
though we

always
had to leave some
on the table, I loved
drinking secrets, eating histories
with you.

HEALING

for CG

The worst pain being past,
the memory of pain comes on:

shame, unjust, supplants
the shouts of anguish you hated

your daughters hearing.
Let them come to the room where you wait

for the next kind of wholeness,
bring what you need. Learn, again, how

to let the body bury its damage,
to walk it slowly into the next room.

LAUGHTER

A thousand-year-old word is like breath,
a hot exhalation

and laughter a part of the human atmosphere
even in grief, in pain.

It wasn't all serious. Or if it was, it was funny
sometimes too—the two things not
exclusive—the best jokes are serious.

Even after it stopped being distraction, a promise,
it remained reassuring. And the glances that pass

between two laughing people, how they link us, even now.

LONG

As I poke a yardstick underneath the stove
to retrieve a kernel of corn that skittered there,
your name, unbidden, is spoken in my mind.

That private whisper of what we long for,
across distances, across a span of time—

a thousand years one word has served them both:
the yearning and the length we yearn across.

YOUNG

It swings like a sling, slung
between two trees, swung
like a child steady enough on her feet

that, grasping a big hand on either side,
she can run up an invisible stair,
step-step-step-step *whee*:

it splays like the waves that keep rolling
in to the beach, or like a bell
that keeps ringing, every peal

a clear new ripple in the air.
This is the word that never grows up,
not in a thousand years.

3

I

I can't see the blood
rising through the
hollow needle
until it begins
to fill the tube,

nor can I see the air
becoming breath
as it's drawn into
the lungs (imagined
as two flaccid
balloons
inflating
around the heart),

or becoming
air again,
unless I were
to stand close
to a mirror,
see a soft cloud
form on the glass,

considering
this body, how
I might know
and not know
what it contains;

considering this word,
another container,
standing upright
on a base,
head open
to be filled.

THOUGHT

Learning to meditate, I imagine my mind
like a balloon at the end of a string.

And, eyes closed, try holding it, not in a fist—
a child's grip, both tight and insecure—

but easily, answering its lift and bob
with my body's wordless gravity.

Yet as a child myself it was easy to lie
back against the Earth, with not just my eyes,

but my mouth, my nose, my belly and chest,
knees, throbbing heart, the whole front of me

looking up, up at the sky,
home of God, receiver of lost balloons.

LOVE

You can hold in your mouth a thousand-year-old word.

Have you ever handled
an artifact that old. Metal bitten by sand.

Wood rotted away. In the Egyptian wing
I thought I would like to hold a shabti,
a humble grave-figure of pottery.

In my mouth this word, love.

How can we fear it does not mean the same?

WORRY

A thousand-year-old word is a nip
at the heel of the mind. The word erodes,
like time itself reshaping paper,

granite, silver; wood-softened corners,
edge-bitten metal. As if the beloved were
an artifact and love a case of glass

sealed in with the only kind of air
that keeps it safe. As if love itself
were not like time in its incessant worry.

LIGHT

I want to tell the dear unborn
about this old word as they rest,
unknown and unremembering,

language coming in like noise,
light like a change in temperature
or an uptick in tempo of the heart,

none of which exists apart from them
as they shift and turn in mute response.
Their mothers' voices are a pattern

of neurons firing. A light behind the eyes.
An old word, but not as old as sun
sliding up a wall or flashing on leaves

or on the hasty braiding of a stream.
Quick flare of a gas stove in the morning,
pale illumination of the moon,

dim glow in the corner through the night—
I want to tell them language can be like light.

UNDERSTAND

Understand the cocoon after the butterfly
has struggled out. A thick scab
starting to peel from a child's knee.

Last night I dreamed we had to move
from a house of sixteen years. But why?

Stand in a mostly dried-up river bed
under a wooden bridge. Look up,
see cracks of sky. Maybe there's no such thing.

Maybe you kneel and turn over a stone,
its loamy underside, the fleeing beetles.
Maybe there's nothing more to understand.

GROW

Spring is afoot. The soft rains come
and we're still here. *Grow*, they command.
The grass green again--overnight, as it it seems,

and it's one of those words that never stops going.
The mouth stays open as it leaves, a soft O,
until the lips close and the breath renews,

though the plum trees, the frogs, and the swallows
have never needed us to say it, not in a thousand years.

CHILD

How can the word be both a kind
of glowing ephemeron
and at the same time so sturdy

Small enough to slip under your shirt
too large to put your arms around

Holding out a pair of hands so dirty
the fingernails are muddy crescents
yet the skin so clean and new

And when you say it sounding
both like a noise of regret
and like a blessing of thanks

NEXT-DOOR NEIGHBOR

Mornings this time of year, we open our windows
as soon as we awake, perforating
our houses. A breeze brings our voices
back and forth, although we are not calling
to one another.

        An unforgiving term,
this phrase that opens like three
panels of ancient wood, hinges
loose on their nails. Whatever was painted there
(a peasant tilling the adjacent field?)
has mostly worn away.

What remains is the nearness—it's always you
we text when, one block over,
illegal fireworks whistle and bang.
A pink tricycle, glossy and bright,
that lies on its side in the grass. A loaf
of banana bread, wrapped in foil, left on the porch.
And the seasons that keep arriving, dawn by dawn.

ACKNOWLEDGMENTS

Grateful acknowledgment is made to Write On, Door County, for residencies where some of these poems were written, and to the editors of the magazines where the following poems first appeared:

"I" (as "The Word I"): *The Inflectionist Review*
"Loss" and "Strand": *The Arkansas International*
"Love": *Poetry Northwest*

Note:
"Kiss": "One easily severs what never was joined" is a translation of a line in the poem "Wulf and Eadwacer."

I would like to thank Laura Reece Hogan and Donna Spruijt-Metz for their readings and improvements of many of these poems, and David Roderick for a thoughtful reading of an early draft of this chapbook. I am grateful to Donka Minkova, Robert Bjork, and the late Marie Borroff for their inspiring teaching of English philology. For invaluable encouragement in their various ways, I also thank Lan Samantha Chang, Matthew Henerson, and Miri Henerson.

ABOUT THE AUTHOR

Nan Cohen's two previous poetry collections are *Rope Bridge* (Cherry Grove Collections, 2005) and *Unfinished City* (2017), winner of the Michael Dryden Prize from Gunpowder Press. Her work has appeared in magazines and anthologies, including *Ploughshares, Poet Lore, Poetry International, The New Republic,* and *Slate.* The recipient of a Wallace Stegner Fellowship, a Rona Jaffe Writer's Award, and a Literature Fellowship from the National Endowment for the Arts, she has taught at Stanford University, Gettysburg College, the University of Southern California, and the UCLA Extension Writers' Program, among other places. She lives in Los Angeles, where she is chair of the English department at Viewpoint School, and directs the poetry programs of the Napa Valley Writers' Conference.

Glass Lyre Press

exceptional works to replenish the spirit

Glass Lyre Press is an independent literary publisher interested in technically accomplished, stylistically distinct, and original work. Glass Lyre seeks diverse writers that possess a dynamic aesthetic and an ability to emotionally and intellectually engage a wide audience of readers.

Glass Lyre's vision is to connect the world through language and art. We hope to expand the scope of poetry and short fiction for the general reader through exceptionally well-written books, which evoke emotion, provide insight, and resonate with the human spirit.

Poetry Collections
Poetry Chapbooks
Select Short & Flash Fiction
Anthologies

www.GlassLyrePress.com